STELLER
Sea Lions

Precious McKenzie

EYE *to* EYE
with Endangered Species

ROURKE PUBLISHING
Vero Beach, Florida 32964

www.rourkepublishing.com

PHOTO CREDITS: © Sieto Verver: Title Page; © Teresa Gueck: 2, 3, 14, 15; © Sue Ding: 4, 5, 6, 7; © U.S. Fish & Wildlife Services: 5; © Associated Press: 7, 19; © Derek Holzapfel: 10, 11; © Kyle Maass: 12, 13, 18, 19; © David Parsons 14, 15; © Craig Lopetz: 12, 13, 23, 24; © Nancy Nehring: 8, 9, 16, 17, 21; © Ujacus: 22; © Dmjunsworth 20, 21.

Editor: Jeanne Sturm
Cover design by Teri Intzegian
Page design by Heather Botto

Library of Congress Cataloging-in-Publication Data

Stearns, Precious, 1975-
  Steller sea lions / Precious Stearns.
      p. cm. -- (Eye to eye with endangered species)
  Includes index.
  ISBN 978-1-60694-402-8 (hard cover)
  ISBN 978-1-60694-841-5 (soft cover)
  1. Sea lions--Juvenile literature. I. Title.
  QL737.P63.S74 2009
  599.79'75--dc22
                                        2009005993

Printed in the USA

CG/CG

ROURKE PUBLISHING

www.rourkepublishing.com - rourke@rourkepublishing.com
Post Office Box 643328 Vero Beach, Florida 32964

Table of Contents

Seals & Sea Lions

What's the difference between seals and sea lions? At first, both animals look a lot alike.

Both sea lions and seals are classified as **pinnipeds**. This means that they are fin-footed **marine mammals**.

Seal

However, there are some important differences. One of the easiest ways to tell the difference between seals and sea lions is to look at their heads. Seals do not have **external** ear flaps but sea lions do. Don't worry, seals can hear, too.

Sea Lion

Seals are usually smaller, shier, and less **agile** on land than sea lions. Sea lions are large, loud, and can walk well with their two front flippers. Sea lions can also move their hind flipper in many directions. Because sea lions move so well on land, many marine theme parks use sea lions in their aquatic shows. However, sea lions are wild animals. And, they can bite!

Seal or Sea Lion?

It has ear flaps.
It is performing.
Then it must be
a sea lion!

Why Are They Steller Sea Lions?

The Steller sea lion was named after **naturalist** Georg Wilhelm Steller. In 1742, Steller sailed with Commander Vitus Bering. They sailed east, from Russia, to discover Alaska. On their journey they found many new and unusual creatures. They named one of these creatures a sea lion because they thought it looked like a lion of the sea.

Sea lions spend much of their time snoozing on rocks near water.

We're Not As Lazy As We Look!

Steller sea lions can swim extremely long distances. Scientists tracked one sea lion that swam 900 miles (1,448 kilometers).

Looking in the Mirror

The Steller sea lion is the largest of the sea lions. Stellers have long, thick necks, two front flippers, and one flexible hind flipper. They also have large eyes and thick whiskers on their snouts.

Do I Have Food In My Whiskers?

Steller sea lions' long, sensitive whiskers help them find their next meal while swimming in the deep, dark ocean.

Adult male Steller sea lions weigh close to 1,500 pounds (680 kilograms) and are about 12 feet

(3.7 meters) long. Males have brown backs and reddish brown bellies. Adult female Steller sea lions weigh a lot less than males. Females only weigh up to 600 pounds (272 kilograms) and grow to about 9 feet (2.7 meters) long. Females are all brown in color.

Their body shape is perfect for diving into the cold ocean water in search of food.

A Land and Sea Habitat

Steller sea lions live in the Pacific Ocean. Their territory ranges from Japan, Russia, Alaska, and south to northern California. But most Stellers are found in Alaska.

Unlike whales, sea lions do not spend their entire lives in the ocean. Steller sea lions enjoy beaches and rocky shorelines.

Stellers spend the summers in exposed areas and then migrate in the winter to areas that offer more protection.

Alaska

Russia

Pacific
Ocean

Japan

**Steller Sea Lion
Habitat Regions**

All in the Family

Steller sea lions live in groups, called harems, which include one adult male and many adult female sea lions.

Steller sea lions are mammals. That means the mothers nurse their **offspring**. Sea lion babies are called pups.

Bathing Beauties

Sea lions raise their pups on rocky shores, called rookeries. Sea lions spend their days sunbathing.

When pups are born they weigh close to 50 pounds (23 kilograms) and most are about 45 inches (114 centimeters) long. All pups are dark brown at birth. To survive in the wild, pups must be quick learners. When they are just one month old they know how to swim.

Who's Barking?

Sea lions are sometimes called sea dogs because they make loud barking sounds like dogs.

Steller sea lions are very aggressive. They often **communicate** through body language. Male Steller sea lions will push and shove to claim their territory. They will also bite one another to prove who is the strongest.

Sea lions can be pushy, but they are also very social animals. They love to gather together in large groups.

Yum!

Steller sea lions are carnivores, or meat eaters. They prefer fish, especially cod, salmon, herring, and flounder. They also dine on octopus and squid. Some will even eat seals!

A Steller can stay underwater for up to 40 minutes while searching for his next meal. But he better watch out because killer whales or sharks might be looking for lunch, and Steller sea lion is a favorite on their menus!

Chew or Swallow?

Sea lions have teeth, but they usually swallow most of their food whole. How's that for good table manners?

Cod

Squid

Salmon

Octopus

Why Are They Endangered?

For the people who lived in the Aleutian Islands, Steller sea lion meat was necessary for survival. Besides eating the sea lions' meat, these people would make clothing and canoes out of their skins.

In the 1960s and 1970s, people began to commercially trap sea lions. They wanted to use sea lions' skins to make coats and boots. This caused a huge decline in the sea lion population. Sea lions became **endangered**. After the creation of the Marine Mammal Protection Act in 1972, it became illegal to trap sea lions.

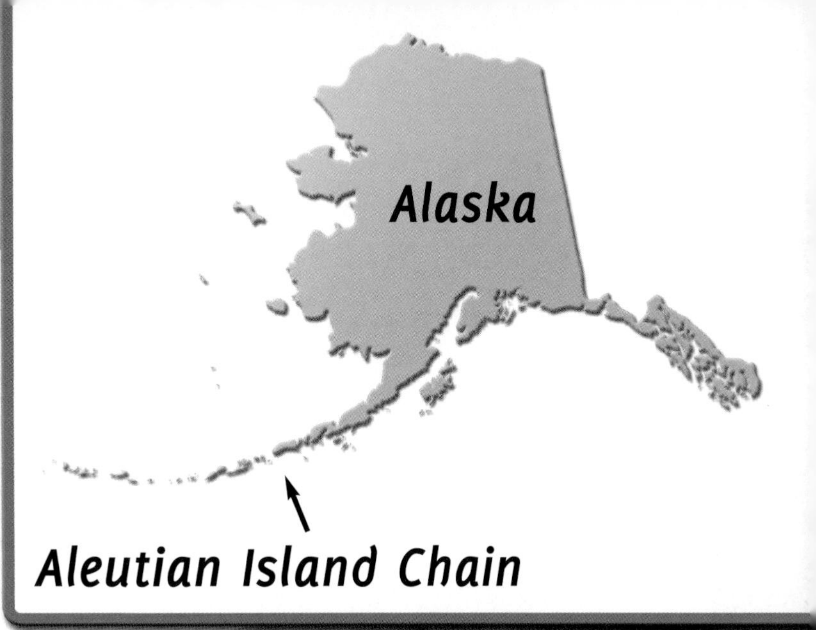

Alaska

Aleutian Island Chain

The Marine Mammal Protection
Act protects whales, dolphins,
sea lions, walruses, manatees,
polar bears, and other
mammals that live in and
around the sea.

Today the biggest threat to the Steller sea lion is man. Commercial fishing has led to the decline of the Steller sea lion population. Fishermen are taking the fish that make up their diet.

Pollution has also hurt the sea lions. Each year, many sea lions become caught in plastic bags and die. Global warming has also affected the sea lions' food supply and habitat range.

The survival of Steller sea lions depends on humans. We must work together in order to prevent the extinction of these beautiful marine mammals.

Glossary

agile (AJ-il): able to move with quick and graceful movements

communicate (kuh-MYOO-nuh-KATE): to share ideas and information

endangered (en-DAYN-jurd): a plant or animal that is close to extinction

external (ek-STUR-nuhl): on the outside

mammals (MAM-uhlz): warm-blooded animals that have fur or hair, a skeleton, and nurse their young

marine (muh-REEN): having to do with the sea

naturalist (NACH-ur-uh-list): a person who studies plants and animals

offspring (OF-spring): a baby of a person or animal

pinnipeds (PIHN-e-PEHDZ): a marine mammal with front and back limbs that look like fins

pollution (puh-LOO-shuhn): poisons and wastes in the soil, water, or air

Index

Websites to Visit

animals.nationalgeographic.com/animals/mammals/steller-sea-lion.html
www.nmfs.noaa.gov/pr/species/mammals/pinnipeds
www.sandiegozoo.org/animalbytes/t-sea_lion.html

About the Author

Precious McKenzie has loved animals and reading all of her life. She was born in Ohio but has spent most of her life in south Florida, traipsing through the Everglades. Her love of children and literature led her to earn degrees in education and English from the University of South Florida. She currently lives in Florida with her husband and three children.